The Little Book of Moon Magic

GH00383840

The Little Book of Moon Magic

TERESA MOOREY

**Andrews McMeel
Publishing**

Kansas City

First published by Ebury Press in Great Britain in 2003.

The Little Book of Moon Magic
copyright © 2004 by Teresa Moorey. All rights reserved.
Printed in the United States of America. No part of this book
may be used or reproduced in any manner whatsoever
without written permission except in the case of reprints
in the context of reviews. For information, write
Andrews McMeel Publishing, an Andrews McMeel
Universal company, 4520 Main Street,
Kansas City, Missouri 64111.

04 05 06 07 08 BID 10 9 8 7 6 5 4 3 2 1

ISBN: 0-7407-4197-7

Library of Congress Control Number: 2004102777

The Little Book of Moon Magic

Welcome to
The Little Book
of Moon Magic!

The Moon is our guide to the realms of
enchantment. Wise, gentle, fascinating, and eerie,
she is queen of the fluctuating forces that govern
our lives. Tuning into the Moon helps us to
harmonize with our own instincts and natural
rhythms. Rediscover what the ancients knew
well—that the Moon rules magic . . .

The Moon's Phases

Become well acquainted with the Moon by
watching her phases and noting how you react to
them, from New Moon through to Full, Waning,
and back to New again. It takes 29½ days
for the Moon to pass through this cycle.

When the New Moon appears in the evening sky,
you can cup the silver sickle in your right palm
in the Northern Hemisphere or in your left
in the Southern Hemisphere.

As the days progress, the Moon rises later
and later, and when she is full she rides
high in the sky at midnight.

When the Moon is waning she can be seen in the
small hours, gradually disappearing into the dawn.

The "Dark of the Moon" is the time between
the disappearance of the Waning Moon
and the reappearance of the New Moon,
when the Moon cannot be seen.

The Moon becomes "new" in the middle of
her dark period. She is invisible at this time
because she is too close to the Sun. We see the
first sickle of New Moon as she begins to draw
away from the Sun at the start of a fresh cycle.

The Moon always keeps the same side turned
toward us—we never see her other face.

Befriending the Moon

Keep a lunar diary to discover how the Moon affects your feelings and actions. In it, note your dreams, how your energy levels fluctuate, your state of health, how much you accomplish, your relationships with others, and anything else that seems important. Make a special note of any intuitive insights or paranormal events.

You may also like to record the reactions of your partner, friends, children, pets, and even plants!

Keep an eye on newspaper headlines— do these reflect the Moon's phases?

After a few months you will come to sense the powers of the Moon and how these powers affect not only you, but the subtle energy field that surrounds us all. Then you will be better placed to use this energy in your lunar magic.

Strange Moons

BLUE MOON is a rare event when a Full Moon occurs twice in one month, with the first Full Moon being right at the beginning of the month. The term is also used for a Full Moon occurring twice in a row in the same sign of the zodiac.

HARVEST MOON is the golden Full Moon that we see in September. At this time of year the Moon rises slowly, hanging close to the horizon for longer than usual. The atmosphere acts like a magnifying glass and makes the Moon look like a great amber balloon.

HUNTER'S MOON is similar to the Harvest Moon, but refers to a Full Moon in October. Stags rut, and there is increased animal activity in preparation for winter.

ECLIPSES occur when the Sun and Moon are in line with Earth. A lunar eclipse happens only at Full Moon when Earth gets between the Sun and Moon, and the Moon appears to turn blood red at midnight. A solar eclipse happens only at New Moon when the Moon gets between the Sun and Earth. Because the Moon is relatively small, solar eclipses are rarely total. Eclipses were regarded as evil portents in ancient times. The Australian aborigines believe that an eclipse of the Moon means that someone on a journey has come to harm.

The Moon's phase and eclipses are noted in newspapers. See how the next eclipse makes you feel.

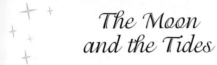

The Moon and the Tides

The Moon has always been associated with water; in fact, the Aztec words for "water" and "Moon" were interchangeable, and even landlocked peoples have often associated her with the fall of dew.

Although the ancient Greeks did not understand gravity, they knew the Moon caused the tides. Many ancient peoples believed that the affairs of humans were also tidal.

High tide arrives with the passage of the Moon overhead, and another comes twelve hours and twenty-five minutes later, when the Moon reaches the opposite point beneath the Earth.

"Spring tides" occur at New and Full Moons. Tides are higher when the Moon is closest to Earth and also at the equinoxes.

While it is unlikely that the gravity of the Moon could affect us directly, there is little doubt that our bodies are "tidal" in a more subtle sense, for life responds to the Moon.

Werewolves and Vampires

A werewolf is a person who turns into a wolf when the Moon is full. Like many myths, this one has a basis in reality, for the Full Moon brings out the wild and instinctual in all of us. It is interesting that this "lunar" creature can be killed only by a silver bullet—the Moon's metal.

Vampires cannot bear the light of the Sun, so must exist by that of the Moon. These mythical creatures embody deep symbolic and psychological meanings. One of the things the vampire represents is all that is pushed into the darkness, but which refuses to die.

Lunar wisdom teaches that we should open our hearts and our imaginations, not to judge but to understand. By being open and accepting, we can enable the things we fear to come out of the shadows, transform, and be reborn, as the Moon is every month.

Living by the Moon

Living by the Moon may mean that your life
runs more smoothly and that you feel healthier
and more energetic.

NEW MOON: Make plans and new beginnings
or make a new start on an established project.
Put new resolutions into practice.

WAXING MOON: Now a project can hit its stride.
Be careful of overdoing things. Direct your
enthusiasm well. Get in touch with friends;
be active. If you need to be on a "build-up" diet,
now is the best time for your body to
absorb nutrients.

FULL MOON: Bring things to fruition and abandon what isn't working. Parties, outings, events, cooking in bulk, lovefests—all go best now.

WANING MOON: Analyze things, shed the unnecessary, have a big sorting-out. A detox or weight-reduction diet will work best now.

DARK MOON: Enjoy a few quiet days; think, reflect, and start to plan the next month.

Gardening by the Moon

Plant life responds to the Moon's phases—
knowing about this will give you a green thumb.

FIRST SICKLE: Plant seeds, especially herbs.

WAXING MOON: Sow seeds over large areas.
Lay turf. Water with special care because now the
absorption of fluids is at its best. Pick fruit and
vegetables that you are going to eat right away.

APPROACHING FULL MOON: If the weather has
been dry, it's best to plant most seeds now.
Water once more. Pick fruit, herbs, and flowers—
they will be succulent. Add fertilizer.

JUST AFTER FULL MOON: Plant root veggies like potatoes and carrots. Plant trees and any flowers except annuals.

WANING MOON: Attack those weeds! Prune trees, mow the grass, start or increase your compost heap. Pick plants that need to be stored.

APPROACHING DARK MOON: Spray fruit trees and cut timber.

Celebrate the Moon!

Need an excuse for a party or outing?
The phases of the Moon can give you ideas.

NEW MOON is a great time for launching a new project, meeting new friends, starting a class, or taking up a new sport or hobby.

FULL MOON is an exciting time for a big get-together. Romances blossom and everyone feels more hyped up. Buy a big bunch of flowers; pour yourself a glass of something delicious, and toast the Moon. Go to a gig or concert and soak up the vibes.

WANING MOON is a wonderful sorting-out time.
Get together with friends to weed gardens, strip
wallpaper, and have quiet time chatting and
relaxing into the evening with close companions.

DARK MOON is a quieter time. You may
choose to spend it with your family or alone.
Light a candle, burn some incense,
and reflect upon your life and your plans.

Moon-Children

Young children are fascinated by the Moon and can learn about natural cycles including the idea of death and rebirth from watching her phases.

Celebrate the Full Moon with a party for any children you know—or just for the child in you! Have a cake with white icing decorated with silver. Light a big white candle. Encourage your guests to talk about the Moon, recite poetry, make up stories, and even to dress up and dance around the garden in the moonlight.

If you are good at crafts, make a cardboard tiara with a circle bounded by two crescents pointing opposite directions to represent the phases. Paint this with glue and sprinkle on silver glitter.

Take turns being Moon Monarch, and perform a little skit.

Kiss Your Hand to the Moon

Kissing a hand to the Moon is an old custom for bringing luck. You can also make the ancient sign of the Horned God (consort of the Moon) by bunching your hand into a fist and then extending only your index and little fingers, so your hand looks like the head of a horned animal. Hold this up toward the Moon so she looks as if she is cradled between the "horns." This works best as a New Moon greeting—a little act of worship that you can follow by making a wish.

Drink to the Moon!

Lemons are ruled by the Moon. Make your own fresh lemonade from organic lemons, using 4 lemons, 5½ oz. golden caster sugar, and 2 pints of springwater. Squeeze the juice from the washed lemons into one bowl and put the empty rinds in another large bowl. Boil the springwater, pour it over the rinds, and add the sugar. Let it cool, strain, add the juice, and chill. Raise your glass and drink down the lunar magic!

Making Moon Cakes

You can make these little cakes to celebrate the Full Moon. Eat them with a glass of white wine or grape juice, and some butter and jam.

You will need: 4 oz. softened butter, 8 oz. golden granulated caster sugar, 2 free-range eggs, 1 tsp. vanilla extract (natural), 1 tsp. white wine or white grape juice, 10 oz. organic plain flour, 1 tsp. baking powder, 1 tsp. salt, 1½ Tbsp. organic honey, 2 Tbsp. quick oats.

Mix together the butter, sugar, eggs, honey, vanilla,
and wine thoroughly. Blend in the flour, baking
powder, salt, and oats. Cover and chill for an
hour, to make the dough easier to handle.
Preheat the oven to 400° F. Roll the dough out
to the thickness of 2 inches and cut into
Full-Moon shapes with a pastry cutter.
Bake for 6–8 minutes, until
pale gold in color.

Delicious!

Moon Meal Celebration

Hold a banquet for family and friends to celebrate a Full Moon. Choose a spread of lunar foods such as milk, cheese, honey, white grape juice, white wine, cucumber, lettuce, white meat such as chicken, seafood (especially crustaceans), white bread, and boiled potatoes. Follow this with a creamy, milky pudding. If you can, use silver dishes, napkins with an appropriate design, and a white tablecloth. Put fragrant white flowers on the table—use your imagination and make your table as "lunar" as possible. Light a white candle in the center in a bowl of water if possible.

Use words of your own choosing, such as "Hail to the shining Goddess; may her light fill our nights, our homes, and our hearts." Each person can have their own saying. Women of childbearing age may wear silver crowns.

Improvise! Have fun!

De-Stress with the Moon

Life in the fast lane can leave you strung out.
Create a lunar haven in your home where you
can relax and be your instinctual self.
All of these can create a lunar ambience:

a fish tank • silver objects • goddess figures
• pastels, blues, greens, and violets • plush
upholstery and carpets • an indoor fountain
• prints and paintings of seascapes and the Moon
herself • crystal ornaments • candles, soft lights
• a tape or CD with sounds of the ocean
• jasmine in an oil burner

Retreat into your haven when the world has been harsh—but don't overdo it. You need to be able to bring your lunar inspirations back to the everyday world if you are to function.

A Lunar Scrapbook

Get in tune with the Moon by
making a lunar scrapbook.

Divide your book into four sections: one for Dark
Moon, one for Waxing Moon, another for
Full Moon, and the fourth for Waning Moon.

Collect pictures and mementos for the four
phases. It doesn't matter whether what you
choose seems sensible as long as it feels right to
you. For instance, you may wish to include a
picture of an old woman in your Waning Moon
section. Some shiny silver coins might go in the
Waxing Moon pages. Or Dark Moon might show
lots of stars, for these are more visible when the
Moon has departed.

Pictures of goddesses and gods can also go in your book, along with poetry, meditations, and spells.

Keep your book safe and secret. Use it to get yourself in the right frame of mind when you do your Moon magic.

An Altar to Lady Moon

Create a shrine in your dwelling to the Queen of the Night. If you need a logical reason, tell yourself you are getting your subconscious self in tune with natural tides. Otherwise, just enjoy!

Select a special shelf and cover it with a silver or white cloth.

Decorate it with silver objects, for silver is the Moon's metal. Animal figures are also suitable. "Lunar" animals include dolphins, bears, dogs, cats, and snakes.

Place candles on your altar. You can choose different colors for the different phases—black for Dark Moon, white for Full Moon, silver for New Moon, blue for Waning Moon.

Figures of goddesses such as Isis or Diana could go on your altar, or the Egyptian Moon-god, Thoth.

Burn an incense stick to celebrate the Moon: jasmine for Full Moon, patchouli for Dark Moon.

Fresh flowers are lovely. A simple goblet of water honors the Moon's tidal power.

Don't be afraid to put anything on your altar that "feels right" to you.

Waning Moon Detox

Have you been overdoing it? Feel that your body is full of toxins? Poisons are more easily expelled as the Moon wanes, so work with Doctor Moon and give yourself a deep cleansing!

Just after Full Moon, cut out meat and dairy; drink at least four pints of water per day; eat organic fruits, vegetables, and cereals; cut out caffeine and alcohol; exercise for twenty minutes a day, and get seven hours of sleep per night.

When the next New Moon comes up you, too, will feel like a new person! Guaranteed!

A Moon Rhyme

Modern Nature worshippers revive the old ways
and often link their celebrations to the Moon, for
she represents the Goddess and shows us the
cycle of rebirth in her movements. Here is a chant
suitable for many festivals, including lunar ones:

We all come from the Goddess
And to Her we shall return;
Like a drop of rain
Flowing to the ocean.
Hoof and horn, hoof and horn—
All that dies shall be reborn.
Corn and grain, corn and grain—
All that falls shall rise again.
Isis Astarte Diana,
Hecate Demeter Kali
Inanna.

Maiden, Mother, and Crone

The phases of the Moon depict the three stages of womanhood. The Maiden is the Waxing Moon, the Mother the Full Moon, and the Crone the Waning Moon.

Many goddesses are linked with one specific lunar phase and one phase of a woman's life. There are also many triple goddesses, such as the Three Graces, or groups of three like that of the Greek goddesses Persephone, Demeter, and Hecate.

At any age in a woman's life she can make contact with any of the three stages, contacting the wisdom of the Crone, the generosity of the Mother, or the freshness of the Maiden— whichever she needs.

Simply use the brilliant Moon as a guide,
and light a candle—white for Maiden,
red for Mother, black for Crone.

Meditate, in the Moonlight if possible, and feel
yourself gently absorbing the special qualities
you require as the Moonlight bathes the sky.

New Moon Ritual to Persephone

Persephone is the Maiden goddess who was abducted by the Greek god of the underworld, Pluto, to be his bride. Her mother, Demeter, the Earth goddess, created winter in mourning. But the gods decreed that Persephone should return to her mother for half the year, and so Spring returns with her.

When you see the first sickle of the New Moon in the sky, light a white candle and burn incense of lavender, lemon peel, and parsley. Have two more white candles with you. Hold up a shiny apple to the Moon or, if you can, use a cut pomegranate instead, for that was the fruit Persephone ate in the Underworld. Say:

"Lady Persephone, as you did eat of the fruit of
fertility so do I, embracing all creative change
that will come in this cycle."

Take a bite of the fruit. As you chew,
light the two other candles and say:

"This one is for what I must remember" and
"This one is for the future."

Relight the candles each evening until Full Moon.
Bury what you do not eat of the fruit.

Full Moon Ritual

You will need a large bowl, preferably made of silver, and a jasmine incense stick. If you cannot perform this ritual outside or indoors where the light of the Moon pours in, use either three candles or one large, thick silver candle as a substitute for the Moonlight.

Burn incense. Look at the reflection of the Moon in the water. Say:

"Lady of Dreams, be my inspiration;
Gypsy of the Skies, be my guide;
Queen of the Night, be my protector."

Drink a little of the water. Immerse your hands in it, then anoint your face, eyes, lips, breast, belly, feet, and any part of you that needs healing. If you wish to become pregnant trace a spiral of the water around your navel.

Pour any unused water onto the ground.

Dark Moon Rite to Hecate

Hecate was a Titaness—a Greek goddess even older than the Olympian pantheon. She was goddess of magic and was believed to stalk the highways and byways when the Moon was dark. Crossroads were especially sacred to her.

You will need a black candle; incense containing myrrh and/or patchouli; a black stone such as onyx or Apache tear; a small silver bowl containing water; and a white candle.

Light the black candle and hold the stone in your hand. As you look deeply into it, think about the month gone by. Do you wish things had been different? What changes would you like to make? Maybe you are happy with the way it went and want things to continue in the same way. Ask Hecate to give you wisdom and self-knowledge.

When you are ready, wash the black stone in the water, light the white candle from the black, and give thanks to Hecate for anything you have realized.

The Moon Rules

Those who work magic believe in a system of "correspondences." This means that if you use substances that "correspond" to your purpose, your spell will work.

Lunar correspondences include:

COLORS: white and silver

HERBS AND PLANTS: eucalyptus, lemon balm, calamus, camellia, camphor, coconut, lemon, gardenia, grape, jasmine, lily, lotus, mallow, Moonwort, myrrh, poppy, sandalwood, willow

STONES: pearl, beryl, aquamarine, crystal, moonstone, sapphire, selenite

METALS: silver

ANIMALS: dog, wolf, dolphin, bear, snake

These correspondences can be used in lunar spells for the home and healing; for children and fertility; or for invoking the imagination, intuition, sleep, peace, or prophetic dreams. Be creative— combine what you need for your purpose.

All is connected in the cosmic web.

Bach Flower Remedies

Bach flower remedies involve using
delicate solutions of extracted plant material
to help emotional problems. Try these
Moon-ruled remedies:

WILLOW: to adjust to misfortune and adversity

ASPEN: to calm vague and unknown fears
you are afraid to talk about

OLIVE: for treating exhaustion or the feeling
that life is without pleasure

VINE: for combating stress, feelings of hardness
or callousness, and the wish to coerce

Witchy Thirteen

Why is thirteen "unlucky" for some but
connected to witches and magic?

The Moon makes thirteen rounds of the zodiac
to each one of the Sun's, meaning there are
thirteen lunar months in the year.

If you are interested in hidden things and magic,
thirteen could be your lucky number . . .

The Moon
and the Zodiac

Just as the Sun passes through all twelve signs of
the zodiac in one year, so the Moon passes
through them all in less than a calendar month.
It takes the Moon just under 28 days to travel
all the way around the zodiac. Because the
zodiac cycle of 28 days is less than the
Moon-phase cycle of 29½ days, each month
the Full Moon occurs in the sign
following the previous one.

The sign that the Moon was in when you
were born is almost as important as your
Sun sign, but to discover your Moon sign
you will need to consult special tables
or get your birth chart drawn up.

Different sorts of magic may be best
undertaken with the Full Moon in a specific sign
of the zodiac—however, you don't have
to wait if your need is urgent!

The Strength
of the Moon

The Moon rules the Sun sign of Cancer.
People born under this sign are sensitive,
home loving, and caring.

Those born with the Moon in Cancer in their
horoscope may have very powerful emotions.

The Moon is exalted in the sign of Taurus.
Those with the Moon in Taurus have stable,
warm feelings and are very faithful and sensuous.

The Moon is in her detriment in Capricorn, which is opposite Cancer. Those with the Moon in Capricorn may be afraid of their feelings, keeping them locked away.

The Moon is in her fall in Scorpio, which is opposite Taurus. Those with the Moon in Scorpio may have very intense feelings that they find hard to express in a positive manner.

Fire Moons

If you were born with the Moon in Aries, Leo, or Sagittarius, you have a fiery Moon. You are enthusiastic about life and have great faith in the future—although when you get depressed everyone knows about it! You have a sense of fun, love a bit of drama, and you are passionate and impulsive. To feel "at home" you need a sense of warmth, stimulation, and meaning in life.

Earth Moons

If you were born with the Moon in Taurus,
Virgo, or Capricorn, you have an earthy Moon.
You are rooted in your body and the evidence
of your senses. You like to be sure of your ground.
It takes you awhile to respond but when
you do, you mean it! Sometimes you can
be a little overcautious. To feel "at home" you
need security, a sense of control,
and knowledge of your resources.

Air Moons

If you were born with the Moon in Gemini, Libra,
or Aquarius, you have an airy Moon. You like to
take life lightly and you are very friendly and
communicative. You may be quick to respond
but you are always just that little bit detached—
you aren't keen to get emotionally involved.
To feel "at home" you need to feel free,
you need truth, and to know all is fair.

Water Moons

If you were born with the Moon in Cancer, Scorpio, or Pisces, you have a watery Moon. Your feelings run very deep and you do not always find it easy to express them—you like to empathize and to feel people understand and care. You can be very emotional and just a touch manipulative sometimes! To feel "at home" you need a feeling of belonging, understanding, and safety.

Zodiac Signs
and Magic

For working magic, the phase of the Moon is generally more important than the sign of the zodiac she occupies. And, although it's easy to check lunar phases in a newspaper, you will need an ephemeris (a list of planetary tables) to know which sign of the zodiac she is in. However, it's easy to work out what sign of the zodiac the Full Moon is in, because she is always in the sign opposite to that occupied by the Sun.
All you need to know is the current Sun sign.
Look at the zodiac wheel and work from that.

If you want to give your magic some extra oomph, work it when the Full Moon is in a good sign for your purpose. But be adaptable! For instance, if you want more mental energy, why wait until the Full Moon appears in Gemini? Use the energies of Full Moon in one of the Fire Signs or in Virgo. You can alter your words to fit.

Moon in Aries Magic

A Full Moon that occurs between
September 23 and October 23 will be in Aries.
Use this time for any magic to do with:

sports, competition, taking first place • having
exceptional energy • facing a challenge,
overcoming obstacles • being brave • starting
something completely new, particularly a new
academic year • healing any ills of the head or
treating headaches

Light a red candle and burn oil or incense
of cedar. Say:

"Aries Moon, strong and bright,
Give to me the strength to fight."

Follow this with words of your own choosing
for your particular intent and finish off
by repeating the rhyme three times.

Moon in Taurus Magic

A Full Moon that occurs between October 24 and November 22 will be in Taurus. Use this time for magic related to:

attracting wealth and material possessions • boosting creativity • enhancing sexuality and sexual attractiveness • the good things of life • security and stability or endurance • helping your garden through the winter months (if you live in the Northern Hemisphere) • healing connected with the neck and throat • boosting the immune system

Light a green candle and burn incense
or oil of patchouli or rose. Say:

"Taurus Moon, riding high,
All good things to me draw nigh."

Follow this with words specific to your intent
and round off your ritual by repeating
the rhyme three times.

Moon in Gemini Magic

A Full Moon that occurs between November 23 and December 21 will be in Gemini. Use this time of sparkle, bright ideas, jokes, laughter, and repartee to:

bring light and life close to you as Yuletide approaches • hold parties • speed the post, make arrangements, swap ideas • improve communication • chat between friends, neighbors, and siblings • work with impartial and detached thinking • travel short distances • heal the arms, hands, and lungs

Light a pale yellow candle and burn incense
or oil of lavender. Say:

"Shining Moon in Gemini,
Light and life to me draw nigh."

Follow this with more specific words
of your own and finish off by repeating
the rhyme three times.

Moon in Cancer Magic

A Full Moon that occurs between December 22 and January 20 will be in Cancer. Use this time of helpful, quiet, and domestic Moon for:

all matters to do with family, children, and fertility • nurturing the imagination, dreams • working with the home, ancestors, and tradition • matters of the sea or safety • holidays and family times in the Southern Hemisphere • healing the stomach, breasts, and the lymphatic system

Light a white candle and burn incense or oil of eucalyptus or jasmine. Say:

"Moon in Cancer, pure and white,
Bring me times of true delight."

Follow this with more specific words connected to your intent and round off by repeating the rhyme three times.

Moon in Leo Magic

A Full Moon that occurs between January 21 and February 18 will be in Leo. Use this time for:

matters concerning power, leadership, success
• creativity, determination • affairs of the
stage and entertainment • romantic relationships
and issues to do with children • boosting
or adding zest to late summer plans in
the Southern Hemisphere • healing the
heart and the chest

Light a gold or orange candle and
burn oil or incense of frankincense,
cinnamon, or orange. Say:

"Leo Moon, I bow to you:
Give me success in all I do."

Follow this with specific words
about your intent and finish off
by repeating the rhyme three times.

Moon in Virgo Magic

A Full Moon that occurs between February 19 and March 20 will be in Virgo. Use this Moon for:

getting organized • having a sorting-out, tidying, cleaning • separating the wheat from the chaff • reviewing what you have achieved • catching up with small jobs and matters to do with your daily routine • cleansing and detoxing of all descriptions • healing the digestive system

Light a green or yellow candle and burn oil or incense of lavender or mimosa. Say:

"Virgo Moon, crystal clear,
All things in their place appear."

Follow this with specific words about your purpose and complete by repeating the rhyme three times.

Moon in Libra Magic

A Full Moon that occurs between March 21 and April 20 will be in Libra. This Moon is good for:

promoting justice and fairness • aiding arbitration and conciliation • resolving breaches and enabling relationships to go smoothly • partnership or legal matters • bonds of love • helping people air their differences and find agreement • creating tact, diplomacy, and balance • healing of the kidneys

Light a blue candle and burn incense
or oil of rose or geranium. Say:

"Moon in Libra, fair to see,
Bring balance, peace, and love to me."

Complete this with words of your own
choosing specific to your cause and finish off
by repeating the rhyme three times.

Moon in Scorpio Magic

A Full Moon that occurs between April 21 and May 21 will be in Scorpio. Use this Moon for:

intense emotional matters such as purging guilt, lust, or obsession • keeping things secret • solving mysteries and getting to the root of things • concentration and exam revision • seeing deep within • dealing with sexual matters • healing the sexual organs

Light a deep-red candle and burn incense
or oil of myrrh or ginger. Say:

"Scorpio Moon, rising from the Deep,
Help me all my power to keep."

Finish this off with words appropriate to
your special purpose and complete it
by repeating the rhyme three times.

Moon in Sagittarius Magic

A Full Moon that occurs between May 22 and June 21 will be in Sagittarius. This Moon is helpful for:

the acquisition of wisdom and understanding • adventures, both mental and physical • travel that truly broadens the mind • expanding the conceptual horizons and getting the "big picture" • long-term planning • "rising above" spirituality • long-distance journeys • healing arthritis and other ills in the hips and thighs

Light a purple candle and burn incense
or oil of clove or sandalwood. Say:

"Archer Moon in Heaven's height,
Help my soul now to take flight."

Finish this off with specific words for your
purpose and repeat the rhyme three times
to complete the spell.

Moon in
Capricorn Magic

A Full Moon that occurs between June 22
and July 22 will be in Capricorn.
This Moon is useful for:

career matters • anything to do with status or
the establishment of a reputation • map reading,
planning, and organizing • binding and grounding
• containing or ending • doing what is necessary
without becoming emotionally incapable
• healing of the knees

Light a dark blue candle and burn incense
or oil of cypress or patchouli. Say:

"Capricorn Moon, bright and round,
Keep my feet upon the ground."

Follow this with special words for
your purpose and finish off by repeating
the rhyme three times.

Moon in
Aquarius Magic

A Full Moon that occurs between July 23 and August 23 will be in Aquarius. This Moon is for wishes to come true and it can help with:

creating detachment • inspiration and keeping a broad, unbiased outlook • humanitarian and charitable matters • telepathy and mental ingenuity • expanding a social circle and getting together with friends • healing problems with the ankles

Light a bright blue candle and burn incense
or oil of lavender or pine. Say:

"High Moon in Aquarius,
Grant me something marvelous!"

Now follow this with specific words of
your choosing and finish the spell by
repeating the rhyme three times.

Moon in Pisces Magic

A Full Moon that occurs between August 24 and September 22 will be in Pisces. This psychic Moon helps with:

the expansion of consciousness • mysticism and understanding dreams—or dreaming true • divination and clairvoyance • escapism and "getting away from it all" • feeling laid back and relaxed • boosting the imagination • healing of the feet or matters involving bodily fluid balance

Light a violet or turquoise candle and
burn incense or oil of ylang-ylang,
eucalyptus, or sage. Say:

"Moon in Pisces, bright your beam,
Bring to me my sweetest dream."

Finish this off with words appropriate to your
specific purpose and complete the spell
by repeating the rhyme three times.

Looking into the Future

If you want to become a seer,
the Moon can lead you!

Take a large, deep bowl of water and sit
with it between your legs, with the reflection
of the Moon falling in it.

Burn a jasmine incense stick, but all
around you should be in darkness.

Take a deep breath, close your eyes,
and frame your question, clearly and simply.

Open your eyes and stare at the Moon in the
water. Look deep, deep within the shining,
mysterious Moon.

The water may cloud over and you may see
figures form. Or you may go into a dreamy state
with pictures forming inside your head.

Be sure to take note of everything you see,
but do not try to work it out—just watch.

Later on you will be able to interpret
what you see and find your answer!

Lunar Libromancy

Need a quick answer to a question? There is a very simple way to divine. All you need is a book and the influence of the Moon's phase.

Choose a general book that covers plenty of life areas—poetry is good, or a child's encyclopedia.

If your question is about outer matters such as "Does he/she love me?" or "Which career path should I take?" choose the time of Full Moon to ask the oracle. If your question is an inward one about knowing yourself and your feelings, such as "Am I really happy here?" or "Can I really trust . . . ?" choose Dark Moon.

Close your eyes, hold the book on your lap, and let the pages run past your fingers until you feel like stopping.

Open your eyes and the first phrase you see on the page will hold your answer.

Boost Your Intuition

Intuition is a natural thing! Candles and
incantations are fine, but we develop true contact
with our instincts by spending time in the places
where they are really at home—in nature.

If you want to deepen your understanding
and development as a seer, take regular walks
when the Moon is in the sky. Look at her—watch
her in all her moods and phases. See how the
world looks when bathed in the silver glow of
Full Moon. Touch trees to see how they "feel"
at Full Moon. Watch the way animals and birds
behave and be aware of the resonance
of the Earth beneath your feet.

Let your inner eye open in response to the Moon!

A Lunar Bouquet

Gather an armful of fragrant Moon flowers to
celebrate Full Moon. Include lilies, camellia,
gardenia, jasmine, poppies, and some sprigs
of willow if you can. All or any will do—include
other white flowers if you like. (Although roses
are strictly ruled by Venus, white roses
may have lunar links.)

Smell the fragrance and draw the subtle beauty
of the Moon within you. Arrange the flowers
on your altar or place them in a shaded corner
of your room to invite the Moon inside.

Moon Runes

In ancient times an alphabet was much more than a collection of sounds. People understood that all is vibration and that in the cosmic spectrum everything is linked. So alphabets had magical meanings.

The Runic alphabet was used by the Vikings, and its symbols were revered. Two runes in this alphabet had strong connections with the Moon:

ALGIZ [Z] links with the yew tree and with the qualities of protection, meditation, and healing. Meditating upon it can give you insight. Focusing on it can help your career, creativity, and friendship, and put you in charge of your emotions.

OTHILA [O] links with the hawthorn and with your home and property. Meditating upon it can help you feel that you belong and help you put down roots. Focusing on it is good for marriage and children and for connecting with your spiritual heritage.

Moon Numbers

Ancient people—and modern numerologists!—believe that numbers do not just convey quantity. They also have a "quality," a vibrational signature, forming part of the cosmic web that surrounds us.

The number two is lunar, for the Moon is the second brightest light in the sky after the Sun, and in her phases the Moon has two horns. The ancients believed that two was a very feminine, receptive number, sometimes subtle and scheming but very sweet and even-tempered.

Each of us has several important personal numbers. You can discover yours by adding together the digits of your birthday (e.g., for the 29th = 2 + 9 = 11 = 1 + 1 = 2), adding up the digits of your entire birth date (i.e., the numbers of the month, day, and year), the numerical correspondences of your name (each letter can be converted to a number, starting with A = 1, etc., up to I = 9, and then starting with J = 1 again).

Do you have many twos in your numerical makeup? Then you are a gentle Lunarian. Any twos in your address or phone number will bring cooperation and domestic balance.

Lunar Alchemy

Alchemy was popular in the Middle Ages,
and lots of mysterious diagrams and writings
on the subject survive, many of which include
lunar symbols. Alchemy was more than an
attempt to turn base metals into gold—
it was a spiritual quest.

The alchemist's power came from the
conjunctio—the union of the king and the queen.
The king was symbolized by the Sun, the queen
by the Moon. This is a reminder to look deep
within ourselves to the balance of male and
female, yin and yang, inside. Without balance
there can be no creativity; without true awareness
of ourselves there can be no progress.

Let the Moon teach you to look within, as she has
taught so many through the centuries.

The Moon in the Tarot

The Tarot can be used for divination and for self-development. In the Tarot, the Moon is card number fifteen of the Major Arcana and it is associated with the astrological sign of Pisces.

The card may appear in any of a multitude of designs, depending on the deck, but it will always show the Moon and may display other associated images such as the sea, baying dogs, or other lunar creatures.

In a spread, the Moon card can mean illusion, confusion, and self-deception. However, reflecting upon this card can help you develop psychism and increase your awareness of dream meanings and your connection with natural rhythms. It triggers an ability to "go with the flow" and to be aware of our roots in the time before time, when instincts were strong.

To make contact with your inner wisdom and to avoid the self-deception that this card can imply, prop up the Moon card where you can see it while you meditate. Light a purple candle and let your awareness deepen.

The Moon
in Your Hand

The mounts on the hand denote certain
characteristics and are named after the planets.

The Mount of Luna, or the Moon, is found
toward the outside of the palm, just above
the wrist, opposite the thumb.

If the mount is high and well formed,
the intuition, imagination, and psychic faculties
are likely to be pronounced.

These characteristics will be even more
prominent if a star formation or other
special marking appears on this mount.

The Line of Intuition—when present—encircles
the mount and signifies marked psychic and
mediumistic ability.

Where the Head Line (the lower of the two
main lines that cross the palm) bends down
toward the Mount of Luna, logic gives way
before the emotions—guard against
depression and illusion and
follow your heart.

Moon Angel

The angel of the Moon is Gabriel, whose
name means "Strength of God."

This archangel is a messenger, awakening us
to cosmic truth, and appears many times in
the Bible as a harbinger of creative change.
Gabriel also parted the waters of the Red Sea
so that the Hebrews could escape from
Egypt, suggesting a connection with the
tides and with passage. Islamic tradition
states that Gabriel, being the Angel of Truth,
revealed the Koran to Mohammed.

Often depicted holding a lily—which is ruled by the Moon—or a scepter, this angel may be male or female. She or he brings the gifts of psychism, seeing, hearing, fertility, and balance. Gabriel comes to us in dreams, whispering those special things we need to know.

Invoke Gabriel with incense or oils of jasmine and/or mimosa, and by wearing a fire opal.

Willow Lore

The willow is ruled by the Moon, and willow roots will often extend far underground in search of water.

This lunar tree is sacred to the Chinese goddess of compassion, Kuan Yin, who uses a willow branch to sprinkle the waters of life.

The willow also signifies death, which is part of the cycle of regrowth.

The tree is also associated with rejection in love.
The custom of wearing the green willow around
a hat when love is lost may originate from
a charm against the jealousy of the Moon
goddess. The Moon is about emotions,
which may be changeable and fickle, and
also about the ways in which we may
deceive ourselves. But on the other hand,
if you want to attract love, carry a willow leaf!

Willow bark and sandalwood may be
burned together as incense under a
waning Moon to call up spirits.

A New Broom

The plant broom *(Cytisus scoparius)* is said by some to be ruled by the Moon. Witches use a besom made from this plant for sweeping out their circle in ritual cleansing before magic.

It was the plant behind the heraldic design of the Plantagenet family, who were said to be involved in the magical arts.

If poltergeists and restless spirits plague you, make an infusion of broom by steeping the plant substances in hot water—the proportions are not crucial. Sprinkle this around your property, saying,

> "Plant of broom so strong,
> Rid me of all that's wrong,
> Keep me and mine safe and sound,
> By your magic all around."

Incense

You do not have to use incense but it often helps to create the right atmosphere for spells if you do.

For your Moon rites, choose a silver censer or heatproof dish for your incense (do not use an old ashtray as this will not be strong enough).

Obtain charcoal discs from a New Age shop. Hold one in tongs, against a flame, until it sparks and begins to go gray. Lay the disc flat in your censer and sprinkle your incense in the center.

A New Moon blend can contain lavender, lemon balm, and calamus.

A Full Moon blend can contain frankincense, sandalwood, and rose (petals or essence).

A Waning/Dark Moon blend can contain myrrh, cypress, copal, and/or orrisroot.

The Olive Tree

The olive is sacred to the Moon, and Gabriel,
the angel of the Moon, is often shown
with an olive branch.

Greek brides wore a crown of olives for fertility,
and olive leaves can be scattered to
bring peace and tranquility.

The olive leaf symbolizes the renewal of life.
Carry an olive leaf for luck and share olives
with your lover, for they are an aphrodisiac!

Magic Monday

Monday is the "Moon's Day"—that is the origin of the name. This is also true in French, *lundi* being the day of *la lune*.

Monday is the traditional day for spells for love and togetherness, for healing hurts, family matters, gardening, travel, anything to do with water or the sea, and for "the sight."

The third hour after sunset is the best time for rituals.

An especially powerful occasion magically occurs if the Full Moon falls on, or just after, Monday.

Magic Circle

All magic is best performed inside a ritual circle,
which gives protection and concentration.

For your Moon magic, make your circle by
directing energy with your forefinger, clockwise,
in a circle around you. Visualize it as blue light.

Your circle should be guarded by the four
Elemental Powers at the four quarters. These
powers are associated with lunar phases:

NORTH is Earth and Dark Moon.
Light a black candle.

EAST is Air and Waxing Moon.
Light a silver candle.

SOUTH is Fire and Full Moon.
Light a red or white candle.

WEST is Water and Waning Moon.
Light a blue candle.

Now you have the symbolic presence of all
the phases and elements to strengthen any rite.
Always mentally dismantle your circle
when you have finished, and give thanks.

(In the Southern Hemisphere, swap the
north/south elements and phases and move
counterclockwise when creating your circle.)

Lunar Togetherness

Have you and your other half been
going through a hard time lately?
Let the Moon bring you close again.

When the Moon is full, fill a large bowl with
fresh water. Add some drops of rose or
jasmine oil, or float white rose petals on top.

Let the Full Moon reflect in the water as you
both sit near the bowl. Put your hands in it
and play with the water and with each
other's fingers. Hold hands, caress,
say nothing . . .

Now begin gently to trace the Moon-water
over the face of your lover—forehead, eyes, lips.
Linger as long as you like, then progress to
other parts of the body.

No need for words—let your fingers
do the talking!

Traveler's Moon

The Moon is a wanderer, but she always returns.

If you have to go far away from home for
any length of time, try this spell to keep you
safe and attached to your roots.

You will need a length of cord, seven
silver beads, seven white beads, and
a large silver candle.

Starting at New Moon, light your candle in
the evening and thread one white bead on
your cord, naming something good about your
home that you want to retain. The next night
thread a silver bead, naming it for something
you hope to gain from your travel. Continue
alternately with each evening that follows.

At Full Moon, thread your last silver bead and knot
the cord around your candle. Let it burn down.

Keep your cord charm with you as you roam—
you will never be far from home.

Lunar Healing

Healing magic is a lunar province.

To send someone well-being, ask their permission to help. Choose a Waxing Moon to work this charm. Anoint a green candle with eucalyptus oil or ring it with a eucalyptus wreath. Imagine the person smiling and joyful. Say:

"As the shining Moon does swell,
So may [name] be happy and well."

You may do this each evening until Full Moon. Then, why not raise a glass of wine or grape juice to the Moon in thanks—along with your fully recovered friend!

Lunar Luck

Know when the New Moon is due to arrive?
It is especially lucky to see it for the first time
over your right shoulder.

Look out for the first New Moon in the New Year.
When you see it, speak your wish out loud—
it will be fulfilled.

The first Full Moon is lucky, too—
it will make your wish materialize
before the year ends.

To See Your True Love

Wait for the first Full Moon of the New Year.
Go out to where the reflection of the Moon
falls on a pool or stretch of water.

Look for your reflection there. Allow yourself
to feel relaxed and dreamy. The face of your
future love will be reflected back at you,
beside your own.

Wishing Moon

Write your wish on a bay leaf when the Moon
is new. (The writing doesn't have to be clear
or detailed—initials will do, as long as you
are very clear about your wish.)

Hold the leaf to your forehead
while you look at the Moon,
imagining your wish materializing.

Sleep with the bay leaf under your pillow.

To Deter Troublesome Neighbors

Take a small hand mirror and leave it out in the light of the Full Moon for several nights until the Moon has started to wane. (It does not matter if the Moon is behind a cloud for much of the time, as long as it has been caught in Moonlight at least once.)

Hold the mirror in your right hand and say:

"Trouble come is trouble turned—
Peace and love to all concerned."

Place the mirror on a windowsill, facing toward your nasty neighbors. Relax! Your shield is in place!

To Find a New Home

When you see the first silver crescent in the sky,
light a white candle that you have anointed
with a little lavender oil. Visualize all the things
you want in your new home. Say:

"Moon, as you sail o'er Heaven's dome,
Spy for me a lovely home
Where I can be happy, where I can rest.
O Wandering Moon, now do your best!"

Light the candle every night until the Moon is full.
Repeat next month, if necessary.

To Break a Curse

In fact, the vast majority of "curses" exist only in the mind of the one "cursed" by reason of their own negativity. Nonetheless, this will help . . .

Choose the first Saturday of the Waning Moon and light a black candle. Say:

"I return all that is dark and evil to this black candle. As it burns down so will all that is harmful to me burn away and be destroyed. Ashes to ashes, dust to dust, so mote it be."

Burn each night until the candle is gone and/or the Moon has disappeared from the sky. Bury any leftover wax in the garden.

Money Moon

There are many lunar spells you can do
to attract wealth.

When the Moon is new, place a banknote of
the largest sum you can afford underneath the
doormat at your front door. Remove it only
when the Moon is full and return it there at the
next New Moon if you like. The larger the
banknote the greater the dividend—and the
more feet that walk over it the better!

Alternatively, place as much money
as you can on your windowsill in the light
of the New Moon. Say:

"O magic Moon, make my money grow."
You can repeat this at the next New Moon.

Folk Spell for Money

When you see the very first silver sickle—
not through glass—turn over the silver coins
in your pocket and say:

"In the name of the Great Mother,
the Horned God, and the Magical Child,
may my money grow this month!"

Now fortune is on its way!

Moonwort
Money Spells

This herb is ruled by the Moon.
Place a sprig of moonwort in your purse
to attract more silver.

Place it in a box at the back of your cupboard
and wealth will come to you.

Burn dried moonwort at the New Moon.
Watch the vapors rise and imagine the wealth
that will soon be yours.

Sandalwood Spells

Fragrant sandalwood is ruled by the Moon.
It is used as incense especially for spells
for healing, protection, and exorcism.
Mix with frankincense for
a Full Moon rite.

Take a large chip of sandalwood and write a
wish on it. Burn this in a heatproof dish,
visualizing your wish as you do so,
to make it come true.

Wear beads made of sandalwood for
protection and spiritual development.
Leave them in the light of the Full Moon
occasionally, for extra power.

Willow Wedding?

Moon-ruled willow can give you an
answer about your love life. To find out
if you will have a relationship over the coming
year, throw your shoe into a willow tree.
You can have nine tries in all, and if your
shoe catches you will be with your love
by the end of the next year.

Give this a try at a party next New Year's Eve—
but remember, you're going to have to
climb that tree to get your shoe back!

Watchful Wintergreen

Wintergreen is a Moon herb, and will
protect children if a little is placed inside
their pillowcase. It can bring them
lifelong good fortune.

Mix it with mint and sprinkle it around
the house to remove bad vibes.

Coconut Nice!

Coconut is ruled by the Moon. Your home
will remain safe if you hang a coconut in it.
But if you don't fancy this hairy ornament,
then cut a coconut in two, drain it and fill the
inside with a selection of protective herbs
such as clove, frankincense, rosemary, mint,
and eucalyptus. Seal it back up and
bury it in the garden.

Workplace Magic

Fed up with the rat race? Would you prefer
to be at home, where it's safe and peaceful?
The Moon understands.

Find yourself a clear crystal. Place it out, or on,
your windowsill, in the light of the Full Moon.
Ask the Moon for calmness and serenity and for
protection from backbiting and office politics.

Next morning take your crystal to work and
put it on your desk. Take a minute to recall the
peace of the Full Moon. Imagine your charged-up
crystal is projecting a force field around you,
like a crystal egg, shielding you from negativity.
Then get on with your work in peace.

Recharge your crystal at each Full Moon.

Waning Moon Spell for Justice

Is someone treating you unfairly or trying
to make you go against your beliefs?
Do this spell at the Waning Moon.

Make a circle of sage leaves, dried or fresh.
In the middle place something that symbolizes
the subject matter, such as a coin for money, ring
for partnership, model house for property, etc.

Sprinkle some sage onto your symbol and
follow with a sprinkle of lavender drops for
wisdom and clear communication. Bind the
symbol round and round with black thread,
seeing your resentment and all the troubles
being "bound up" along with it.

Leave this on your window ledge until the first crescent of the Moon appears. Take it outside and unbind it, seeing all the negative issues take flight. Bury the cord in the ground along with your symbol—or if this is to be used again, wash it in a running stream. Go forward with a clear head and light heart.

Salt Spell for Protection

The Moon-ruled sea is salty, and salt has many ritual uses involving cleansing and protecting.

Fill a clear vessel with springwater and leave it out in full sunlight and the light of the waxing Moon for a twenty-four-hour period.

Now dissolve some salt in the water.

Sprinkle this in the four corners of the room that needs to be protected. Sprinkle it also around the window and door.

If you need to protect an entire apartment, house, or garden, sprinkle the mixture around the boundaries.

Lunar Love Spell

When the New Moon appears in the sky find
a heart-shaped petal, preferably of a rose.

You will need some red or rose-pink paper
and a silver pen. Write on the paper:

"As the fair Moon waxes to full,
My true love to me I pull."

Have a bath or shower and put on
a clean robe—or stand naked.

Light a rose-red candle and chant your
words three times while you hold the petal
in the candle's glow.

Fold the paper around the petal and seal it
with some of the wax from the candle.
Place the paper somewhere safe.

By the time New Moon arrives again,
love should have come, too.

Beauty and the Bath

Need a special boost for an important date?

Choose the time when the Moon is
just approaching full. Light six candles
in silver holders around your bath.
Three candles should be rose pink, three white.
The bathroom should be warm.

Drop some rose oil and/or sprinkle
rose petals onto the surface of the bathwater.
Burn a rose-scented incense stick or
place more of the oil in an oil burner.

Soft, sensuous music will help you relax. Close your eyes and imagine that your body is absorbing radiant beauty from the surrounding water. Just feel yourself glow! Imagine as many seductive situations as possible, where the lover of your dreams is totally smitten by you.

When you are ready to get out, wrap yourself in a huge, soft, rose-colored towel and get ready in a leisurely way, knowing that delights are to come!

Anger Begone!

Choose a Waning Moon for this spell and,
if you can, stay up until you can see the
Waning Moon in the sky.

Burn a black candle. Write down all the things
that are making you angry on a piece of
white paper with a black pen. Get it all out!
Then twist the paper into a taper. Think of how
good it will be to be free of these thoughts.

Light the paper in the candle flame and place it
in a strong dish—preferably black—to burn.

Carefully take the ashes out and cast them
at the Waning Moon, saying:

"Old Moon, on the wane
Take away my ire and pain."

Sprinkle a little lavender oil on your pillow
and imagine all the good things to come
as you fall asleep.

White Wash

Are you dashing around too much, not giving
yourself time to think, feeling cut-off,
confused, and stressed?

When the Moon is full and fair, take a
white satin scarf out into the moonlight.
Hold it resting on your arms. Face the Moon
and close your eyes.

Feel the light of the Moon wash through you,
cleansing away all the stress, muddles,
and anxiety. Let your mind go blank,
breathe deeply, and take the lunar glow
deep inside you, opening your mind,
making you calm and receptive.

Drape the scarf about you, come back inside,
have a milky drink, and wind down—
do nothing for the rest of the evening.

Wear the white scarf whenever you
need to chill. Recharge it with the
same ritual next Full Moon,
if you need to.

Faeries by Moonlight

The Irish know faeries as "the People of
the Sidhe"—beautiful and terrible creatures
from another dimension. It is a great privilege
to see faeries: Do not be afraid but
be very respectful.

One of the favorite traditional times to see
faeries is by the light of the Full Moon.
When the Full Moon shines on the trees of
the Faery Triad—the oak and ash and thorn—
then you may be especially likely to
glimpse the Fair Folk.

A garden full of fragrant roses is sure to appeal to faeries—look for them at midnight by the light of the Moon.

But if you fear seeing the Little People when you have to go outside when the Full Moon is gleaming, then carry a sprig of gorse for protection.

Moon Stone—
Beryl

Crystal balls used to be made
of this Moon-ruled stone.

Beryl can be worn to keep you safe
when traveling by sea. It guards against
drowning and seasickness.

Wearing beryl can help you resist manipulation
and coercion by salesmen and evangelists.

Five hundred years ago, it was believed that
beryl could help the wearer win debates and
still be liked and respected by all!

Beryl is exchanged by lovers so that
their love may remain true.

Moon Stone—
Chalcedony

This milky white stone is ruled by the Moon.

It brings peace, calms fears, and cheers
the heart when held or worn.

It wards off black magic and all negativity.

It is especially useful for nursing mothers,
who can wear beads of chalcedony
to help stimulate the flow of milk.

Moon Stone—
Crystal

There are many types of crystal, and it is,
of course, the favorite substance for the
"crystal ball," although balls for divination
can also be made of glass or of other stones
such as amethyst. White, clear crystal is
especially powerful for Moon magic,
especially when set within silver.

To make your own miniature circle of power,
choose a variety of white crystals and
embed them in white or silver sand
in a large dish. Or, if you are quite sure
of your final design, you could set them
in self-hardening modeling clay.

For your design, you could set the crystals in
the pattern of astrological symbols such as
a crescent for the Moon or the "female" sign
of a circle with a cross beneath for Venus.
Or just do whatever feels right for you.

Use your crystal temple to "charge" objects
that you are going to use magically, such as
charms and amulets. For instance, a piece
of rose quartz set within the Venus sign
and left out in the Full Moon would make
a wonderful love charm.

Moon Stone—
Geodes

All crystals take shape within geodes,
which are hollow, often egg-shaped structures
that may be very beautiful. They may be
quite expensive, but they make wonderful
ornaments and magical objects.

Keep a geode in your bedroom while making love
if you want to have a baby, but take it out before
sleeping, as crystals can be powerful things.

Use a special geode as a focus for meditation,
catching the flickering candle's glow—
amethyst is especially good for this—or place
one on your altar to amplify your energies
when doing magic. A geode on a lunar altar
is a perfect way to honor Lady Moon.

Moon Stone—
Marble

Marble is made of lime and shares some similarities with coral. Marble is a protective substance. Place some marble on your altar if you are doing spells to shield you from attack of any sort, or carry a piece that you have "charged up" by either leaving it in the light of the Full Moon or in a magical rite.

Marble is good for kitchen fittings as it brings the right lunar "vibe" for cookery, domestic arts, and security. Work surfaces with a marble finish aren't quite the same, so add a real marble chopping board for greater effect.

Moon Stone— Aquamarine

This blue-green stone has links with the sea.

Leave an aquamarine in a clear glass of
fresh springwater in the light of the Full Moon
for several hours. Take out the stone with
clean fingers and sip the water to cleanse
you inwardly and to prepare you
for magic or divination.

Moon Stone—
Moonstone

Obviously with strong lunar associations,
moonstone's powers are so linked to its
namesake that these gems are said to wax
and wane with the Moon in the heavens.

Moonstone is sacred to the Moon goddess,
and many witches like to wear it. It can be
placed beneath your pillow for a restful sleep
and sweet dreams. A moonstone necklace
can be worn in bed.

It is also protective and can be given to
your friends when they go off on a trip,
especially if traveling by sea.

Hold the stone in your hand as the Moon
is waxing to full. Visualize the lunar power as
a white light that beams down, surrounding
the little stone and causing it to pulsate with
protective energy. So great is the survival
power of this little stone that the bearer
cannot possibly come to harm!

Give it with love—and ask for a
postcard in return!

Moon Stone—
Mother-of-Pearl

This isn't really a "stone," but the interior of
the shells of sea mollusks. Avoid commercial
mother-of-pearl because the creatures will have
been killed to obtain it. Collect your own,
if possible, in rock-pools and streams.

Empower a special piece of mother-of-pearl
to give as a protective gift for a newborn baby—
or you could simply use a clean seashell.

When the first silver sickle appears in the sky,
face the Moon and hold up your piece of
mother-of-pearl, visualizing the sparkling light
entering it. Feel it tingling with power. Say:

"New Moon, as you grow and shine,
so may this little one grow and thrive.
Blessed be."

Give it, wrapped in white satin,
to the parents.

Moon Metal—
Silver

Silver has long been sacred to the Moon.
Witches and priestesses often wore silver
crescents in honor of the lunar Goddess.

Silver reflects negativity away from the
person who wears it, just as the Moon reflects
the light of the Sun. The "horns" of a
silver crescent repel evil.

Silver is related to love, healing the emotions
and psychic abilities. Wearing silver may
attract love, but it can also cause you to
feel emotionally overwhelmed at the time
of the Full Moon; wearing gold can
balance its effect.

Silver set with a stone ruled by the Moon is a powerful lunar charm. Those touched by silver are able to shed anger and nervousness. A silver ring can keep you calm.

Silver jewelery helps you sleep, especially if set with moonstone. It can give you psychic dreams. Silver may also be placed beneath the pillow for the same effect. This metal also guards travelers, especially those at sea.

To Get Rid
of a Problem

When the Moon is waning, write your problem on
a piece of paper and burn it. Simple!

To End a
Run of Bad Luck

Check the Moon phases in a calendar or
diary and time this spell so the last day you
do it falls on the last day of the waning Moon.
Each day go for a walk and pick up a piece
of dried wood. Do this for seven days.
When the Moon is at her darkest, bind the
twigs with black thread and burn them. Say:

"Ill luck, your time has come to die;
A bright new phase is drawing nigh."

Lunar Law of Magic

Moon will wane and Moon will grow:
"Harm none" is the one rule you must know!

*To see the Moon wax and wane, flick through
this book from back to front if you live in
the Northern Hemisphere, and from
front to back if you live in the Southern.*